Paul Blackburn

FEARLESS
Mastering The Monster

FEAR IS WHAT DRIVES EVERY STRUGGLE YOU HAVE

Quantum Orange Pty Ltd

ISBN: 978-0-6455480-2-0

First published 2016

Copyright 2016 - 2023 Paul Blackburn and Quantum Orange

quantumorange.com

DEDICATION

This is for the child within all of us who would rather that fear didn't exist.
It's for the dreamers who imagine being courageous against all odds.
It's for those who would do great deeds if they could overcome their doubts.

This book is dedicated to everyone who has ever asked God or the Universe to send hope that they could overcome their limitations and become the person of their dreams.

WITH SPECIAL THANKS TO

Mary Blackburn. Thank you for teaching me that there is something deep inside of me that is loveable and worthwhile and for your constant, tireless support for my crazy ideas over 41 years of marriage. Without your willingness to do whatever it took to find whatever I needed at the drop of a hat, this (and many other projects) would have withered on the vine.

Emma Thomas. Thank you for going the extra mile under difficult circumstances - you've become the only editor I will ever entrust with my raw manuscripts. As a team we are up to book number six and you continue to grow into the role in such a way that I've started to look at the finished products and wonder if they're more of a collaboration of two authors than the work of an author and an editor.

Julie Blackburn. Thank you for your dedication to holding fast to our values and beliefs in both our business and personal lives. Your never ending love is one of my greatest gifts and your willingness to shoot for the moon and not accept second best has made me a better man.

Angela Melit. Thank you for being the client from heaven. Your willingness to act on your intuition, follow your heart and make a genuine difference in your profession is inspirational. Thank you for making sense of the concept that fear has an actual location in the body.

IT'S NOT YOUR **FAULT!**

You were most likely born in fear.

If you were your mother's first child, the pain was more than she had ever experienced. Even if your birth was perfect, your early life was far from it. Your parents lived in a world full of background fear.

Their reactions and responses to that fear were accepted without judgement by your open and fresh mind. Though you may not have understood it, you were totally aware of what took place in your home and subconsciously made note of it.

Those impressions converted to beliefs. The beliefs became indisputable facts.

And those facts are consistently reinforced by the way you interpret your life experiences through the filter of your beliefs.

Meanwhile, your mother's love for you (immense as it may have been) didn't hide her worries, struggles, concerns and fears.

It's highly likely that your personal fears are reflections of or reactions to those harboured by the significant figures in your early life - be they openly displayed or secretly suppressed.

Background FEAR.

As a baby boomer, my teenage years were influenced by the Beatles and The Rolling Stones re-inventing rock 'n' roll.

Lurking in the background was the probability of mutually assured destruction of the whole planet. Nuclear warheads were numbered in the thousands on both sides of the Cold War. Kennedy and Krushchev played brinksmanship on a monumental scale. We were reminded on a daily basis that the world could end soon.

It's not hard to understand how we became practiced at absorbing a high level of background fear.

But does the world really look much different today?

Will you be beheaded by a religious zealot who lives quietly and unobtrusively down the street for 10 years before running amok? Will the 'plague' re-emerge because of our dependence on antibiotics? Was the world financial crisis in 2008 just a warm up for the real thing? Will we die of thirst or hunger because of global warming?

In clinical work we see two major groups of people - those who are carbon copies of their parents and those who are the complete opposite.

Take a moment to reflect on the following statement: *"I am determined to be nothing like my father!"*

It won't be long before you realise that this person created exactly what they wanted to avoid, simply by focusing far too much mental energy on it.

And although our history plays an important role in the way we deal with fear (or don't!), its only a small part of the story. Personal change would be easy if we only had to deal with our parent figures! Unfortunately, the entire western world thrives on fear, propagates fear and reacts to fear.

Take the evening news as a minor example creating mass hysteria. A stunningly handsome or beautiful face delivers an account of the day's disasters. If there are insufficient local scoundrels to warn us about - they will actually go overseas to get enough tragedy to fill up the half hour.

Meanwhile, childhood passes and we carry the limitations created in that time forward.

We become adults convinced that:
> Speaking in public is equal to or worse than death

> Snakes are evil creatures plotting to eat your children
> Failure is personal, permanent and shameful
> Loneliness is a fault to be hidden
> Pain is to be avoided at all costs
> The unknown is too frightening to contemplate
> Rejection is a sign of your fundamental (unfixable) faults
> Heights create the desire to jump
> Death is too scary to talk about...

...and a thousand other fears known or unknown to us.

We become superbly qualified at avoiding the circumstances that exacerbate the fear. When the teacher is casting around for someone to give a speech in class we shrink - we literally make ourselves smaller by sliding down in the seat, hunching our shoulders and staring at the floor. We avoid starting anything (procrastination) because if we haven't started then we can't fail. Some people even stay away from balconies, fences, glass lifts, cable cars or elevators that open onto the top of a building. Since we successfully avoid 'facing the fear', we never become the master - remaining the slave for the rest of our lives.

For much of our waking day our subconscious is on alert. The possible 'embarrassments' may never eventuate but we are nevertheless ready. This constant state is called hyper-vigilance and is the real reason so many of us get to the end of the day exhausted.

Our system exacts a toll for such high energy activities, which is why a day where nothing goes wrong can be as taxing as one where everything goes completely haywire.

It all boils down to this…

What saves us as a child, imprisons us as an adult.

FEARLESS

LOVE IS LETTING GO OF **FEAR**

Did you attend a class in school called *"Your Emotions And How to Handle Them"*?

Probably not, which is a crying shame because emotions drive so much of what we do and most people are completely clueless when it comes to handling them properly.

What follows will explain 90% of human behaviour - especially your own. Let's start with this...

There are hundreds of emotions. Some are single feelings like sadness, others combinations of many emotions. For example, sometimes sadness is just that, pure and simple. On other occasions sadness is tinged with regret and perhaps remorse. Or we may even experience sadness coloured with loneliness, feelings of unworthiness and the question of whether we have any friends at all.

These hundreds of feelings (and their combinations) are all legitimate expressions of our emotions. Unfortunately, the plethora of possibilities pretty much muddy the water when it comes to understanding and managing our emotions.

With that in mind, we're going to focus on what is known as the six basics. The theory is that all emotions are, at one level or another, versions of these six basics.

The six are: Joy, Peace, Love, Anger, Sadness and Fear.

People act differently when you display them. Simple observation in our early life means we learn that exhibiting joy, peace or love gains us positive responses such as acceptance, companionship, loyalty and friendship.

During the same time we come to understand that outbursts of anger, openly shedding tears or displaying fear results in people engaging in conflict with us, suddenly becoming busy or disappearing completely. Those negative responses teach us that anger, sadness and fear are not okay.

Despite no one ever siting us down and saying, *"It's okay to be happy, peaceful or loving but you shouldn't be angry, sad or scared"*, we learned it as sure as if it were tattooed on our foreheads.

We need to grasp one concept - it is a critically important, game changing realisation. It will most

likely run counter to your established beliefs, but try entertaining the idea for long enough to test its validity.
The word emotion is a contraction of energy-in-motion.

We don't think emotions - they can only be felt. When an emotion is 'up' we experience it both as a feeling and as a physical sensation.

For example...

When we're angry, we'll often feel a swell of energy coupled with a 'tightening up' of our muscles. Clenched fists are a common clue.

Sadness causes both an energetic and physical 'collapse'. Look for feelings of overwhelm, heaviness or depletion, coupled with doubling over and holding the face or stomach.

Fear, quite simply, paralyses. We feel dread and lose the ability to think, breathe and move. Muscles become incredibly tense and 'lock'.

Notice the lack of thinking in those examples? It is simply not possible to think through a feeling. We can only feel our way through it.

The critical concept referred to above boils down to this: the undeniable truth is that the healing is in (the expression of) the feeling.

That's the basis of this work. When we can safely express what has been bottled up inside for years, there is immediate and permanent relief, followed by genuine change for the better. The only alternative is to suppress our emotions, which is extremely unhealthy.

Suppression

Any emotion restricted in its movement through your body has to go somewhere.

As children, we intuitively know this and freely express ourselves. Those around us who are unsettled by our 'outrageous' behaviour shut it down with whatever means fall to hand.

These same people will be unable to explain why they were out of line or why they were so compulsive themselves.

All we need to know is that the suppression adds up. When the container can hold no more - there will be sporadic but increasingly common 'eruptions'. The three so called negative emotions start acting up on us!

Anger builds to the point that a ballistic launch happens over a trivial event. Sadness accumulates until bursts of tears become a regular event and sufficient fear causes panic attacks.

To the un-initiated, these behaviours are signs that they're 'losing it' and heading closer to madness than they ever thought possible. All that's needed is a dose of emotional expression and equilibrium will return.

To keep moving forward, let's look at those six basics again.

Joy
Peace
Love
Anger
Sadness
Fear

If you had to eliminate one from each of the two groups of three - which would it be? Your decision should be influenced by what you think is the most superficial in each group. Put a line through either joy, peace or love and another line through anger, sadness, or fear.

Most people will end up with a list of four that looks like this...

Joy
Peace
Love
Anger
Sadness
Fear

Anger is fast and easy to fire up, but also dies back quite quickly. Joy is much the same.

Now perform the same exercise again. Remove one from each group because you consider it to be less 'important' than the other.

Joy
Peace
Love
Anger
Sadness
Fear

We eliminate peace, because love is more fundamental. If we love enough, we'll find peace as a result. Therefore love is more important. Sadness gets crossed off because it's personal - it's about 'me' and something that's been lost. The loss of that same thing may not make another person sad.

The two remaining emotions are love and fear. If we look at them closely, it becomes clear that they're almost opposites.

Love is the absence of fear and fear is the absence of love.

That's a very powerful concept, especially when applied practically. Let's look at an example…

The fear of speaking in public is incredibly common. When I'm speaking to an audience of around 400 people and ask if anyone in the room has a fear of public speaking, a forest of hands rise. I pick someone and ask them to come up on stage - they arrive visibly shaking, breathless and bright red.

We talk about the feelings and sensations they're experiencing and how long the fear has been there. Eventually I ask what they're really afraid of. Ninety percent of them say they're terrified they'll make a fool of themselves.

Next, I ask them to imagine that they've been given thirty minutes to live. If that were true, what message would they want to leave with their loved ones, perhaps even the world?

The same person who was petrified two minutes ago is suddenly committed and passionate. They begin talking powerfully, capably and impressively.

What changed?

The depth of love tapped into by imagining that scenario overcame the fear of being on stage. Fear vanishes when we find love.

Love is letting go of fear.

FEARLESS

THE BRAIN - BEST ASSET OR WORST ENEMY?

Though there is some debate about a total average number, experts agree that a normal adult will have a minimum of 20,000 thoughts per day. Those thoughts range from a couple of words right through to long sentences connected to a central theme.

Given the sheer volume of contribution, it's not hard to see how the voice in your head can be either your best asset or worst enemy, especially when it comes to working with fear.

The chatter created by that voice is commonly known as 'self-talk'.

Research has shown that the majority of self-talk is negative and is therefore working against you, not for you. Those negative thoughts consistently create anger, hopelessness and fear.

Meanwhile, there's plenty of research to support the fact that positive self-talk creates better results. When you're aware of what you're thinking, you can revise the thoughts that don't serve you and replace them with phrases that empower you. At the very least, positive self-talk will help you better manage whatever situation you find yourself in, including those in which you find yourself scared.

Clearly, you need to do whatever it takes to shift your pattern of negative self-talk into something more constructive. It is critically important that you begin training your brain to be your servant, because the only other option is it working against you.

Positive versus negative aside, there are a few major issues with self-talk you'll need to sort out before you can expect much success in dealing with fear. Let's have a look at them...

Self-Talk Issue #1

We simply aren't exposed to the idea that we can train our self-talk into a pattern of our choosing. We don't question the thoughts that pop up, calling them out as ridiculous and of no consequence. We just accept them as they are.

As a result, the brain becomes unruly and undisciplined, throwing silly concepts about demanding we treat them seriously and throwing tantrums if we don't. We end up with immature minds that chatter away endlessly and unproductively.

A staggering number of people tell me they have trouble sleeping because they can't shut their mind down. They feel like they don't own their brain, their thoughts just attack them and they're powerless to stop it. Equally numerous are those who share that they've tried meditation a few times and it just doesn't work because their mind is too active. The unspoken implication is that they're too smart for simple meditation.

In both of those cases, what we're seeing is a childish brain that has fallen in love with itself. This brain is so self-centred that the idea of training the brain has never even occurred to the person who is supposed to be in control of this potentially wonderful asset.

Self-Talk Issue #2

Since we don't question the thoughts that pop into our heads, we don't challenge them either. For most of us, there's only one voice up there and whatever it says that appears reasonable, we run with. Our capacity for critical thought is drastically diminished when it comes to self-talk.

Here's an example of an unquestioned train of thought. This type of thinking is very common and might take hours or minutes - but notice the lack of counter argument…

"I think I need a new car."
"Probably the old one has things going wrong that I don't know about yet."
"This one is getting a bit on in miles and years, how long have I had it again?"
"Did I just hear a rattle in the suspension over that last bump?"
"I'd better look at getting a new car sooner rather than later then."
"I wonder what's good value for money in cars at the moment."
"Maybe one of those hybrids would save me some money."
"Oh, the current car runs out of registration soon."
"I wonder what I'd get for a trade in on this car."
"Only one way to find out I guess, I'll call in at a dealership to have a look around."
"Love my new car."

Where was the thought that the current car just needs a good service? Or that new suspension would cost thousands less than a new car and gain several years life in the current car, saving money overall?

Self-Talk Issue #3

Thoughts build momentum and get distorted to such a degree that your memory of an event that happened 20 years ago is likely totally inaccurate. In fact, it probably only bears a passing resemblance to what actually took place. Why?

We distort things gradually. We don't remember an event as it was, we remember it as we last remembered it. If the memory is altered by one percent each time it comes to mind, it won't take long before the situation being recalled is barely recognisable.

The same is true for other thought processes - they tend to distort and reinforce along the way.

Self-Talk Issue #4

We automatically assume (most often incorrectly) that others are thinking along the same odd pathways we do. That is, we project. Unfortunately, we rarely know we're doing it and it damages us, our relationships and our ability to succeed significantly.

For example, I once had a client spend an hour telling me about his disastrous breakup with the girl he intended to marry. It was tumultuous, torturous and expensive. I noticed that he was reciting the story, not expressing any emotions. I asked what he was feeling.

Client: *"Feeling? What the hell do you think I'm feeling? Are you a total moron?"*

Me: *"If I were you I'd be feeling relieved that it only cost me fifty thousand to get rid of the bitch. After all, that is what you called her isn't it?"*

He assumed I'd be feeling the same loss and grief he experienced and was quite shocked when I pointed out I wasn't. Any person listening to that story would have thought he was better off without her, but he simply couldn't see that.

Clearly we're in desperate need of serious, productive brain training to overcome the bad habits we've developed by not paying enough attention to what the naughty child living upstairs is doing.

So, now that the idea has occurred to you, how do you go about training your brain to be an asset when dealing with fear?

Here's a few techniques you can (and really should) try...

MEDITATION

The list of scientifically proven benefits of meditation is enormous. We won't list them here - suffice it to say you absolutely need to be meditating regularly.

There are many forms of meditation, each with something different but equally beneficial to offer. It's worth trying them all, including the physical forms like yoga and tai chi.

Meditation is a technique you'll need to persevere with if you want to reap the rewards. In the beginning it can seem like progress is slow, but stick with it and meditation will become a powerful positive force in your life.

As the Dalai Lama says, *"After years of meditation as a means of claiming and training my mind, I am beginning to get the hang of it."* That's how much there is to gain from meditation - you'll still be gaining new insight 40 years down the track.

Commit to meditating regularly and your life will change forever.

BRUSH OFF NEGATIVE THOUGHTS

This process was originally a Buddhist idea and is particularly useful for dismissing thoughts that are not constructive. When an unhelpful, negative or nasty thought arrives, simply say, "Not that thought" as you brush it off. Some people find it helpful to move their hand in front of their face as though waving the thought away.

Let that thought go and refocus by saying, *"The thought I would rather have is..."*

This technique is absolute gold. It doesn't stop negative thoughts, but it prevents them wasting your time and energy. The brain will gradually come to understand that particular thoughts just aren't getting any traction and will stop sending them, so the number of negative thoughts you're having will reduce dramatically.

TURN AWAY FROM NEGATIVE THOUGHTS

This technique is similar to the one above, but more physically pronounced. Some people respond better to turning their back on a thought than brushing it off.

When a thought you don't want pops up, physically turn your body around saying, *"I turn my back on this thought and all others like it - don't bother sending thoughts like this."* Then you can move to the preferred thought.

MANTRA

A mantra is a short statement with deep meaning repeated over and over, most often used to create spiritual awareness. It works by taking up conscious brain space so the practitioner can focus on the assigned meaning.

I suggest choosing a word or phrase for yourself to use as a mantra when needed. It may have significant place in your religion, be an emotional state you wish to embody or even be a series of sentences that take concentration to say in the right order. Whatever you choose, the trick with a mantra is to give it meaning and then repeat, repeat, repeat!

One of the greatest rugby league goal kickers of all time once told an audience he mutters 'black dot, black dot, black dot' while he is placing the ball, stepping out his run, lining up and taking his shot. Of course, the black dot his mantra refers to is the painted patch marking the middle of the cross bar. Simple, meaningful, powerful.

Here are a few examples of spiritual mantras:

God is love.

I am love.

I am at peace.

Every day in every way, I am getting better and better.
I am all that I can be.

This one that has, without fail, pulled me out of the 'real world' since 2003...

"I give thanks for this day to the great spirit whose presence and perfection I feel within and without. I still my mind and emotions in order to practice the six perfections of gratitude, wisdom, discipline, patience, enthusiasm and compassion. May my heart be opened and my mind enlightened such that I experience genuine health, wealth and happiness."

AFFIRMATIONS

Affirmations work in much the same way a mantra does, but tend to have a lot more words. When using affirmations, choose words you find inspiring and uplifting and then put them in sentences that describe you in the best possible way.

For example...

I am powerful, successful and fearless in the face of anything that turns up in my life.

Success comes to me easily in everything that I do. I seem to have a natural talent for doing and saying the right thing to get me where I want to go.

Affirmations can be repeated silently in your head,

stated out loud, read in front of the mirror or even written down. Like a mantra, affirmations require repetition to work effectively.

GRATITUDE JOURNAL

Take a few moments each day to write down what you are grateful for. If you're not sure what to write, start with the fact that you woke up this morning when many others didn't and go from there. Include everything you can think of, big and small.

This is an immensely powerful way to teach your brain to focus on the positive. The impact a gratitude journal has on your thinking, and therefore your world view, is extraordinary. Try it before you dismiss it as mere positive thinking.

MINDFULNESS

Mindfulness has a similar positive impact to meditation, but you can do it in small bursts all day long. All you have to do is pay complete attention to what you're doing in the moment, to the exclusion of all else.

Thich Nhat Hanh wrote an excellent book, The Miracle of Mindfulness, which I'd highly recommend reading. In it he talks about how the washing up is either a chore to be finished quickly or a meditative activity rewarding on its own. He talks about, *"... feeling the texture of the water, its temperature, the touch sensations of the cutlery and crockery, the slipperiness created by detergent..."*

You can do this with any activity you're undertaking throughout the day. I'd recommend finding at least five ten minute spots you can practice mindfulness in. The benefits are extraordinary.

WHAT IS **FEAR**?

We are not taught to ask: *"What is the good purpose of this... thing/event?"*

As a consequence we fail to realise that even the negative emotions serve a helpful purpose. Sure, that positive origin more often than not becomes distorted by an inability to properly handle emotions, but it's there.

The primary function of fear is to protect. It warns us when something is not right or we are in danger. Fear of being burnt is the reason we're unlikely to hold a hand on a hotplate, which is a good thing.

For survival purposes, fear runs through the amygdala or 'primitive brain', which processes information far quicker than we can think. It is lightning fast, reactive and completely unresponsive to logic. The amygdala will have the heart pounding, lungs powering and sweating started long before we know what the particular threat is. This is the reason we can be filled with terror before we know what's going on.

For example, if you have a fear of snakes and someone throws a rubber one at you, your primitive brain will have you responding with fear before your rational brain can observe that the snake is not a real one.

The fact that fear does not respond to logic is something we struggle with because we don't like not being in control. For those scared of speaking in public, no amount of rationalising stops the brain numbing panic induced by imagining a hostile crowd.

It's for that (and many other) reasons that we arrive at the default conclusion that fear is bad and must be made to go away. Mood altering substances and activities enter the picture and stay. There are hundreds to choose from, but the most popular in Western cultures is alcohol. It's cheap, easily available and does exactly what people hope it will - inhibits fear.

This is why drunks fight and karaoke bars are popular. The very person who couldn't sing two notes at a morning meeting is likely to be the one keeping everyone entertained with 'just one more' sung horrendously loudly and seriously off key.

The problem with these consciousness altering drugs and activities is that they wear off. When they do, the fear is right there waiting like a faithful puppy. Except that the puppy has grown up and is now a wolf capable of devouring dreams.

Fear promises to save us…

"Don't go out there in front of that crowd. Stay here with me, where it's safe."

But that promise is empty. Fear does not keep us safe. At best it is an imposter masquerading as a master of keeping us safe. While we sit down the back of the room, shrinking physically to avoid being picked to speak in front of the crowd, we're actually experiencing what fear promised to save us from: the terror that someone will look around and select us next.

The impression that fear creates within us is that we won't survive the circumstances we find ourselves in. That's why issues that seem small can bring us undone - they trigger a larger fear.

The trigger (heights, speaking, spiders) may be small, but it taps into our fear that we won't survive (fear of death) and suddenly we're a quivering mess.

Just one of the many processes for handling fear is to ask:

"What is the positive purpose of this emotion?"

For many people, that simple enquiry is enough to trigger a disconnect from the primitive brain and therefore leave the fear behind like a warning sign on the highway.

WHAT HAPPENS TO **UNRESOLVED FEAR**?

We know that unresolved fear gets stored in the body, but what exactly happens to it? Where does it go? What impact does it have? And more importantly, what can we do about it?

Liz Koch, author of The Psoas Book, proposes that the primary muscle involved in storing fear in the human body is the psoas. The psoas is a long muscle that fans out from the T12 vertebrae, connects to the five lumbar vertebrae and then attaches to the pelvis and top of the femur (thigh). The psoas is the only muscle that connects the spine to the legs - it is what holds us upright and enables us to walk. The psoas is the principle muscle associated with physical stability.

In addition to connecting the legs and spine, the psoas is also connected to the diaphragm. Since that's where we control proper breathing, it's also one of the locations that the physical symptoms of fear manifest. That is, when we're scared we often stop breathing.

The psoas muscle is also intimately involved in the fight or flight response - it can curl us into a protective ball or flex to prepare the back and legs to spring into action at a moment's notice. Unfortunately hectic modern lifestyles drain us physically and mentally, which prevents us from naturally releasing the stress we've built up. This keeps us in a state of fear and anxiety, which in turn locks the psoas muscle into a constant fight or flight response.

Obviously there are strong, multi-directional links between the psoas muscle and fear. Of particular note is the clinical observation from body workers like Koch that fear is very often over-represented in people with a constricted psoas muscle. Since fear is an emotion that can 'lock' itself into the body and the psoas muscle is also prone to 'locking' when chronically stressed, it's easy to see how the two mechanisms feed one another in creating additional (unnecessary) fear and anxiety.

In talking about the research indicating that the psoas is vital to our psychological wellbeing as well as structural health, Koch states that the psoas, "*...literally embodies our deepest urge for survival, and more profoundly, our elemental desire to flourish.*"

Because the psoas is so connected to our basic physical and emotional reactions to life, a chronically tightened psoas leads the body to believe it is in danger, eventually exhausting the adrenal glands and depleting the immune system. When the fight or flight response is continually engaged, contact with the inner self (and therefore the ability to identify and process fear effectively) is lost.

The lifelong stress often placed on the psoas in Western cultures leads to many problems, both physical and mental. Physically, a chronically stressed psoas can cause back, hip and knee pain, digestive issues and breathing dysfunction. Mentally, psoas issues can have an impact on our view of the world, emotional well-being, interpersonal relationships and general sense of happiness. Koch states, *"Whether you suffer from sore back or anxiety, knee strain or exhaustion, there's a good chance that a constricted psoas might be contributing to your woes."*

Given all of the above, it's not hard to conclude we need to be paying a lot more attention to the health and wellbeing of the psoas muscle. If we can rebalance to the muscle, we can release the tension stored there. Doing so will have a profound effect on our physical, mental and emotional well-being, as well as create greater ease in releasing fears.

Koch says, *"As you learn to approach the world without chronic tension, psoas awareness can open the door to a more sensitive attunement to the body's inner signals about safety and danger, and thus to a greater sense of inner peace."*

So, exactly how do we go about releasing the psoas muscle?

Getting started is actually simpler than you might think. I have a client named Angela who has spent over thirty years working as a physiotherapist treating psoas muscle problems. She's shared an excellent technique for a basic psoas muscle release with me. Here's how it works…

Get The Patient Into Position

The patient needs to be lying on their back, with both knees bent up at about 45 degrees, feet flat on the floor. Eyes should be looking directly at the ceiling, shoulders down and relaxed, hands lying by the sides with palms facing up.

Place a 20cm very under inflated soft stability ball (Pilates ball or similar) under the mid back. That is, a little above the belly button, just underneath the edge of the sternum. Check that the neck is in alignment - a book may need to be placed under the patient's head to ensure it's not tipped back.

This pose does mean the hips are in flexion, but they're not in full flexion. The idea is to position the muscles such that they are in the middle of their normal, natural range of motion. Nothing is stretched, because the idea is to create a release, not a stretch.

Focus On Breathing

If a patient has been locked in fear or pain, turning on the psoas muscle has most likely become a habit. Since the diaphragm is connected to some of the places the psoas muscle is as well as the psoas itself, focusing on the breath is a key element in creating a psoas muscle release. Simply put, placing the muscle into a relaxed position and focusing on the breath gives the muscle the signal to start releasing.

The patient needs to focus on breathing into the area where the psoas muscle is. If there's pain there, they can breathe into the pain. If there is no pain, the patient can simply focus on breathing into and relaxing the area.

Relax & Hold

It's important to note that this exercise is not a stretch - it will not be effective if held for thirty seconds. The patient needs to relax into the position described above and breathe into the area for a minimum of five to ten minutes in order to create the release.

If the patient experiences one sided tightness or discomfort, which is common, gradually move that foot out to lengthen the leg a little and continue the breathing.

If there is no discomfort, the patient can eventually straighten the legs out and breathe into the exercise from a more lengthened position, which is very advantageous. If not, just keep the knees bent - the technique will still be effective.

Roll To Get Up

This is critically important - if the patient sits straight up they will turn the psoas muscle back on and undo the release just created. The patient should roll onto their side, get onto all fours, pull the hip in underneath themselves and then stand up.

This is a quick, easy and immensely powerful exercise. It's effective at releasing all types of fear, including any background fears you weren't aware of. I highly recommend you do it regularly.

For more information on the psoas muscle or the technique above, contact Angela's clinic on the details below.

Pain Slayers Physiotherapy
Graceville, QLD
www.gracevillephysio.com.au
07 3278 1186

FEARLESS

YOU WERE TAUGHT TO BE AFRAID

Given that pretty much everyone is afraid of something, there's a good chance you were negatively influenced by watching your parents, relatives and/or teachers fail to deal with fear appropriately. In short, you would have seen scaredy cats masquerading as brave and fearless warriors. This is, of course, very confusing for young children.

You could have witnessed anything from Uncle Joe standing speechless on a chair because a mouse entered the room, to Mum losing sleep for a week because she had to read the minutes at the P&C committee meeting.

These are relatively easy concepts to deal with. You can write Uncle Joe off as a bit weird and Mum is just Mum. What's not obvious is that both Mum and Uncle Joe are suffering from two kinds of paralysis.

The first is that they were powerless to affect the situation. The demonstration we get of an adult being controlled by their circumstances is not lost on us. We don't think about it in words, but our observation is that even adults (super humans in our young minds) can't change the way things are. That is a life lesson that stays with us forever.

The second is that both Uncle Joe and Mum were resigned to the fear being a fact. Their only defence was to make the fear 'go away'.

For Uncle Joe, jumping on the chair achieved little in terms of alleviating the fear, but there was no chance of getting him down without displaying a dead mouse and taking it outside.

Mum just went quiet and suffered her way through it, hoping it would end soon and that no one would ask her a question during the meeting. As a child, you probably didn't notice her tossing and turning in bed or having an extra glass of wine with dinner, but subconsciously you'd have been aware something wasn't right.

In short, the lesson demonstrated by the people you considered powerful was 'do whatever makes the fear go away'. It's highly likely you never witnessed someone tackling a fear and overcoming it by working through it in some kind of ordered process. You didn't see someone feeling empowered and victorious - there was not a demonstration of finding resolution.

At best, you might have had some well meaning person tell you to 'face your fears' - that speaking in public is the answer to a fear of public speaking and standing on a cliff edge cures a fear of heights. That strategy does not overcome fear. It just causes more trauma by suggesting the ridiculous idea that you can summon enough courage to bully fear into submission. Perhaps if you ate concrete for breakfast and nails for lunch, by some miracle you'd toughen up enough that the fear would bugger off because you threatened it with a shellacking.

What a preposterous idea. Fear suddenly gets scared of you?

Doubtful.

Sadly, the only possibility when using the 'make it go away' strategy we're all taught is that the fear gets suppressed. By puberty, we're experts at not displaying our emotions - anything unexpressed gets pushed down and now resides in the body somewhere.

Unfortunately, successive suppressions add up. You're likely reading this book because the sum total of all the suppressed emotion is now greater than the vessel holding it. The emotions start to bubble over, erupting unannounced with virtually no triggering event. Faced with that, most people come to the conclusion that they're losing it.

With the education outlined above, we are left with no choice other than minimising the tumultuous times created by going anywhere near our fears. In short, we become experts at avoiding the things that trigger us.

But none of this is a real fix. It's simply the management of a problem that will never be resolved.

The already murky water is further muddied because fear is also used in a variety of ways to affect our behaviour. Politicians tell us we'll end up living in caves if we vote for the other side, the police take our money if we speed and we'll never find a partner if we don't buy the special toothpaste so we can have perfectly white teeth.

Fear plays so many roles in our lives that we never think to question its validity. We just assume that we have to react to it or suffer more trauma. The idea that we could work with fear and get somewhere with it never occurs - mostly because we are surrounded by people who have made no progress themselves.

The nearest you'll have come to a successful fear eradication technique was no such thing. Let's have a look at why it has failed so many people...

You were likely instructed that you could 'get used to it' (and therefore no longer fear it, apparently) by taking small steps. For a person afraid of speaking in public, the encouragement would be to start with just two or three people. Then six or seven, next perhaps ten and obviously one day, a football stadium. For someone scared of snakes, watch a snake show from the back row. Read all about them. Next sit in the front row at the snake show, maybe even touch a harmless python. Before you know it - become a snake charmer and handle cobras.

This process is even has a name. Progressive Desensitisation.

Paramedics and pilots alike are trained in simulations and situations that become steadily more stressful. Once they can handle an engine or a heart stopping, they can pay attention to the fuel or blood pouring out. Then smoke filling the cabin and the spectators starting a fear fuelled riot, all while they stay calm and keep working.

Sadly, many a potentially great pilot or paramedic never even considered the job because of an untamed fear of heights or blood. The problem with Progressive Desensitisation is that it is not resolution. It is simply a 'trained in' failure to respond to emergency signals generated by the body. The subconscious brain 'freaking out' doesn't stop. It gets suppressed and will return one day. The problem is that when it does, our bodies will have cooked it into something nasty. It will be enormous, out of control and near impossible to deal with.

The suppression of everyday fears (so that we can function normally) becomes a routine affair. Unfortunately, we don't realise we're filling a finite tank and at some point it will have to overflow. In the current climate, that won't take long to happen because the level of background fear in our culture is higher than ever. Many people don't even know what they're scared of, they just wake up with a feeling of dread.

Perhaps that feeling of general, background fear is what has sent you looking for a book like this one. Or maybe you've got a specific fear you're ready to conquer. Either way - congratulations! You've discovered a way forward that will leave you empowered and victorious.

As with all personal journeys, the reward for overcoming that which you were previously unable to is beyond measure. You won't just get what you want (the fear eradicated), you'll be introduced to a more powerful, capable and courageous you. Most importantly, this version of you will be sticking with you for the rest of your life.

Overcoming whatever fear has brought you here is just the beginning, because you'll be learning to learn. You'll come to realise that we are the only species on the planet that can change the chemical composition of our brain.

All of that is possible just by changing the way we think and the actions we take with regard to our previously rampant emotions.

And that, my friends, is a truly miraculous idea.

Let's jump into exactly how to do it…

FEARLESS

THE BLOCKAGE BUSTER TECHNIQUE

For over thirty years, this has been one of our most effective techniques for dealing with fear. Simply put, the blockage buster technique works. It is a 'fix it and go' process.

When we implement it with participants in live workshops, it is normal for us to get two people processed in about thirty minutes. We'll generally have someone previously terrified of heights out on the balcony at the top of the building, while simultaneously having someone petrified of speaking in public up on the stage in front of 200 people laughing, joking and teaching what they have learned so far in the program. These participants tend to be people who've held that fear for over twenty years and they move forward without the fear returning.

A shift that big in such a short time can be difficult for those with chronic fears to comprehend. Their fear has been so powerful, so debilitating, so persistent and gut wrenching that a half hour fix seems too big a leap.

But give it a go before you write it off. If you don't get a breakthrough with this technique almost instantly, simply apply it again to gain permanent victory. At first, the process is best performed with a friend leading you through the steps, but once you are familiar with them you can use it on yourself at any time with outstanding results.

Here's what to do...

STEP ONE - Identify the feelings

Sit down somewhere quiet and take a deep breath. Find the feelings (close your eyes if you need to) and describe them as fully as possible using as many words as you can. If writing is something that works for you, grab a pen and paper and get your description written down.

The idea is to articulate your feelings so effectively that anyone hearing what you're saying would understand exactly what you mean and be able to empathise. If fear arises while you're working, do not stop the process. Just describe the sensations and feelings.

A few tips:
- Avoid using short sentences or phrases
- Stick to describing emotions
- Avoid 'reasons why' - they are not relevant

- Start with the physical sensations
- Observe without judgement

STEP TWO - Locate the feelings

Find the place in your body where the feeling lives and put your hand on it.

Decide quickly and intuitively or your rational brain will attempt to take over. Just get a sense of the place where the feeling seems to come from or be the most intense.

STEP THREE - Explore the feelings

The next step is to explore the feelings you've identified. With your hand remaining in position over the feeling, begin asking questions about it. You're looking to get to know it.

Here's some of the questions we use:

- What colour is it?
- What shape is it?
- How much water could it hold?
- Is it light or heavy?
- Is it moving or still?
- What does it want to do?
- Does it have a name?
- Would you be willing to let it go?

Once you've reached a place where you're ready to let the fear go, move to step four.

STEP FOUR - Welcome the feeling in and let it expand

Take a deep breath and welcome the feeling. This will feel counter-intuitive and you may experience resistance.

The idea is to welcome the feeling in, give it a right to be there and let it expand. Actively encourage the feeling to grow. Breathe into it, giving it nourishment and letting it move or expand how it wants to.

You may feel overwhelmed, like you're drowning or being engulfed by the enormity of the feeling. Just hang in there.

NB: You do not have to suffer. You can simply observe what is happening.

STEP FIVE - Emptiness

At the point where overwhelm seems imminent, the feeling will gently vanish. Most people describe an emptiness where the feeling was, but are not really aware of it unless asked.

STEP SIX - Choose a feeling to fill that position

Nature abhors a vacuum and will quickly fill it with whatever is handy. Before the fear can refill its previous position, decide what feeling you would like to carry around in its place. Anything like love, peace, joy or confidence will work beautifully.

Actively fill the empty space with the new emotion. Feel it expand into the space and lift your spirits.

Take a few moments to welcome that new feeling to what will be its permanent home.

STEP SEVEN - Check if there's more

We often waste a lot of time trying to move past a surface feeling (without much success) not knowing that there is another, more powerful emotion that needs to be healed residing underneath it. This second or third layer of emotion can cause us real problems if left unhealed.

NB: This step won't always be necessary when using the Blockage Buster Technique - in many cases you'll be able to complete the healing process with step six.

When you feel like there's more work to do, here's how to do it...

1. Look for the recurring feeling.

2. Once you find it, lock your attention onto it and put your hand on the part of your body that the feeling seems to be emanating from.

3. Ask yourself what the feeling is.

4. Once you are clear on the initial feeling, ask yourself what is underneath or driving that feeling. It is often helpful to ask, 'I am feeling this way because...'

5. When you identify the emotion that is underneath the original, you are close to the real driver of the behaviour that bothers you. Explore this feeling as extensively as possible using the process outlined in steps one to six of the Blockage Buster technique.

That's it - one of the simplest and most effective techniques for overcoming fear.

Why does it work?

In short, because it allows the fear to do its job.

When we push feelings down, they fester and

create problems. In the case of fear, it promises something that it doesn't deliver. Like a nasty little goblin in your ear it says, *"Stay here with me, don't go up there and do that. If you stay with me you'll be safe, I'll protect you from embarrassment, shame, guilt and feeling generally awful."* In truth fear, embarrassment and shame are what it delivers.

What the blockage buster technique does is allow the fear to run its course. Since the fear was just trying to warn us of possible danger, it got to do its job when it was welcomed in. The fear therefore serves no further purpose and dissipates.

Like all emotions - fear turns into a giant if suppressed but simply vanishes when properly felt.

FEARLESS

THE REFRAMING TECHNIQUE

Anthony Robbins would call this technique a 'pattern interrupt'. It works by breaking the habitual cycle that the brain runs in. Once that cycle is broken, we have the opportunity to choose something else.

Robbins' version of a pattern interrupting technique is excellent. Typically he will bring someone afraid of public speaking up on stage and ask them about their current state. Of course, they're terrified and stammer out words to that effect. When they're halfway through explaining how they feel, he'll ask where they got the clothes they're wearing from. Since the interruption is sudden and completely unexpected, most people just answer the question. Doing so snaps them out of their state of fear - they get lost in telling the story of finding the outfit and forget their surroundings. It often takes several minutes for them to realise they're standing on a stage chatting away comfortably in front of thousands of strangers.

Our version of a pattern interrupt technique works in a similar way, but is based on a different concept. Rather than encouraging getting lost in own our reverie, the reframing technique pulls us into the moment. This is a very powerful concept.

Here's a practical example…

When I ask someone afraid of public speaking onto the stage, the conversation generally goes something like this:

PB: Hi Fred, using that microphone in your hand, tell us how long you have felt this way.

FRED: Um, since like I was, um maybe a teenager?

PB: Great, would that be 20, 30, 40 years?

FRED: Uh huh.

PB: So is that more like 20 or 40?

FRED: Yes. Oh, I see. Um probably 25.

PB: Can you remember this fear ever not being there?

FRED: No, it feels like, um, it's been there forever.

PB: Cool. So I assume it has stopped you doing much in the way of speeches etc?

FRED: Argh, yes, I think, um this is, um my first speech ever.
(He and the crowd laugh)

PB: What else has this fear stopped you from doing? When you look at the overall impact on your life - what opportunities has this fear stopped you from taking up?

FRED: Shit. I never thought of it like that. Massive. Yeah - too much...

PB: Tell me Fred, what is it that you are actually afraid of?

FRED: All those people staring at me.
(Looks at crowd nervously)

PB: Look at the crowd again please mate. Just look at their faces. Tell me again, what it is you are actually afraid of?

FRED: That I'll make a fool of myself.

PB: Okay. While you are thinking about that - who is the centre of attention in your mind?

FRED: Well, um, me, I guess.
(Looks surprised)

PB: Take another look at the crowd for me again and tell me what they are all attending this workshop for. What do they want to get out of this weekend?

FRED: I suppose they are all here to learn.

PB: Great, you got it first go. So let's do some teaching. Would you be up for that if I helped?

FRED: Um, I suppose…

PB: What's the stand out key learning that you have got from the two days so far? That is, what's the bit that you know beyond any shadow of a doubt, that if you take it home and used it, it will transform your life?

FRED: Oh well that's easy. It's super important to meditate every day. Don't miss a day and if you have a chance, meditate for a second time.

PB: Sweet. When should you meditate?

FRED: Definitely before you leave the house each morning. If you have to get up 15 minutes earlier each day to fit it in, just do it because the results will be worth the effort.

PB: Is there anything you should include in the meditation?

THE REFRAMING TECHNIQUE

FRED: Absolutely - it's really important to make movies of you reaching your goals. Just string the movies together - they only have to be a few seconds long. You should include as much detail as you can.

PB: Awesome. Any hints to make it work better?

FRED: Yep - you have to pack as much emotion into it as possible because pictures and feelings are the language of the subconscious so the movies will 'stick' better if they are full of feeling.

PB: Mind if I take over before the crowd asks you to stay and me to go?
(Fred and crowd laugh)

Why does this technique work so well?

Because fear can only exist if you transport yourself into the future. To be afraid, you must have left the present moment. Bringing yourself back into the present loosens the grip of fear because the truth is, right here in this very moment, you're fine.

Fred was afraid of what might happen, not what did happen. His imagination had spun the whole story into a disaster in which he was going to be publicly humiliated. The fact that his mental 'picture' of events may never happen is a truth he had chosen to ignore. The emotion (fear) is a response to his choice to live in the future rather than the present.

In any set of circumstances that are creating fear and drama for you, one great solution is to bring yourself back into the present moment.

The reality is you can be right next to a snake and if it hasn't bitten you yet, then everything is going well. Allow your mind to shift into the future and you may well be dead from heart attack a long time before the snake becomes a real threat.

Another practical example is a visit to the dentist, where the most frightening location in the whole place is the waiting room. Most people who are scared of the dentist allow the fear to take control when they hear the drill running. What they fail to realise is that the drill is currently in someone else's mouth - absolutely nothing is going on in the waiting room.

Fear is all about what might happen, not what is happening right now. Let your mind wander into the future and you'll be terrified in no time. But here's the key point - you don't have to be thinking about the future.

THE REFRAMING TECHNIQUE

The mind is extremely capable of coming back into the moment. We just have to remind it who is in control. Sure, it can come up with a hundred scenarios in which you get damaged, but did you ask it to do that? When it does create calamities, do you tell it to stop misbehaving? Or do you just complain that it does it and stand by helplessly waiting for it to come up with something else?

A wise person will train their mind to be their servant and not accept the rubbish that it can (and will) serve up.

FEARLESS

FINDING **FEAR**

For the past 100 years or more psychologists have been convinced that the best way to treat fear is to find the traumatic experience that was the initial cause of the fear. That is, if we learn you were attacked by a dog as a three year old, then we'll have figured out why you have such a profound fear of dogs. The automatic result of this discovery is somehow meant to be that your fear is suddenly and magically cured. Voila!

There's never been a practical explanation of how discovering the original dog attack liberates the person experiencing a fear of dogs. In truth, 'Why am I like this?' is a question not worth bothering with, but we spend many frustrated years with it because we have nothing else to work with.

Here's a snapshot of the ridiculous mental battle the 'Why am I like this?' question creates...

One you: Why do I have this thing about dogs? I love animals. Maybe I'm just not a dog person.

Another you: It's because you were scared almost to death by a dog that wanted to eat you.

One you: Why did the dog do that though?

Another you: Maybe you were being unkind to it.

One you: But why do I get the shakes when a tiny dog snarls at me? Surely I'm losing it. I'd better keep this to myself - people will think I'm nuts for being scared of a Chihuahua. And I'll keep it really quiet that despite being terrified I really really want a dog.

Another you: You should get some help - I'm stuck in here with a crazy person.

One you: That dog nearly had me! Why wouldn't the owner stop laughing? They should have been helping me, I was clearly terrified!

Another you: I don't know why people are rude like that. But could you please be quiet? You sound unhinged.

One you: Oh my gosh, look at those little twits stealing a street sign! If I caught them I'd set a pack of dogs on them...whoops...bugger it, I do sound crazy!

That type of conversation runs through your head on a semi-regular basis for as long as the fear of dogs goes unhealed.

Clearly, we don't need to know why we are the way we are - we need to know how to get better. We need to know what to do to begin the healing process. Emotional exploration is a lot like a television crime show - we take the clues in front of us and work out what's next.

As an example, let's take a look at what properly exploring a fear of dogs is like when I sit down with a client...

Me: How can I help you Fred?

Fred: I completely freak out when I see a dog off lead, even if it's a long way away. I'm sick of it.

Me: Okay, does that urge have a name that is also an emotion?

Fred: What do you mean?

Me: Well, an urge is a very strong feeling. It's important you know what the feeling actually is because it's creating the need to come and see someone like me. What's driving the urge?

Fred: (Thinks for a minute). I guess it's fear. I just want to run and run and not stop. I don't know why you're talking about urges, I just came to see you because I'm desperate to stop feeling like I'm out of control. And I'm furious with dog owners in general, they're a careless bunch of people.

Me: Okay, bear with me here. How long have you had these feelings?

Fred: As long as I can remember.

Me: Is it the dogs or their owners?

Fred: All of them. The dogs should all be locked away so we can feel safe. Crap, what did I just say? Am I crazy? But seriously, why couldn't we just get rid of all the dogs? Oh bugger, this is confidential right? I don't know why I'm like this. Please make it stop!

Me: That's the problem Fred, you've been trying to make it go away for years.

Fred: This is nuts. It doesn't make any sense at all. Clearly I've lost the plot.

Me: Just hang in there. You've been suffering for 25 years, surely you can handle five more minutes...

Fred: Okay. What do I have to do?

Me: Find the anger. Where does it live in your body?

Fred: (Looks startled). What? Are you crazy? (Angrily) What do you mean?

Me: Now that you are angry, put your hand on the part of your body that the anger is emanating from.

Fred: (Puts hand on stomach). Okay.

Me: Feel the anger surging.

Fred: Uh huh.

Me: What's 'under' it? What is the feeling there that's deeper than the anger?

Fred: Pain, hurt. Anguish. (Tears running down his face)

Me: Expand on that more for me - say more about it.

Fred: It feels like pain that won't go away.

*We will need to come back to this pain and heal it.

Me: Good. What will happen if the pain continues as it is?

Fred: I won't survive it, it's too big.

Me: Tell me what it feels like.

Fred: I'm scared. No - I'm terrified! Why am I scared? Where did this come from? What am I supposed to do?

Me: How old do you feel right now?

Fred: Three or four. Wait, what? What's going on? What's that got to do with this?

Me: At that age, and feeling this way, what decisions did you make about yourself?

Fred: I'm not big enough, I'm not strong enough, I don't know what to do. I'm alone and no one will help me.

We could continue, but the picture is pretty clear. Fred's entire life has been characterised by not being strong enough, by feeling alone and like the world in general wants to hurt him. As a male in Western culture, he's been taught to keep all of those feelings to himself and pretend confidence and capability. He has no idea why he has difficulty with dogs and their owners.

The question is this...

Does Fred really need to know about the original dog attack or does he need to know how to fix what remains within him as a result of that event?

Obviously the second option is going to be far more constructive for Fred since it will allow him to move past the fear and get on with life. The most effective tool to use in this type of situation is the Blockage Buster technique, which has it's own chapter in this book. In Fred's particular example, step seven would be crucial.

Essentially, Fred needs to turn towards the feelings and welcome them in, one at a time. As he allows each feeling to simply exist, exploring them with curiosity, he'll heal himself and open up to new possibilities in his life as a result.

FEARLESS

PROLONGED **FEAR** SEQUENCES

An emotion prolonged (suppressed) becomes a mood.

A mood prolonged becomes an attitude.

An attitude prolonged becomes a view of life.

We could use any emotion as an illustration of that sequence, but sadness gives an excellent demonstration.

Sadness occurs when we have lost someone or something of value, turns up in waves and generally manifests as tears. When allowed to run its course, sadness eases of its own accord because it has been expressed and is no longer being carried in our physical system.

Since we don't normally have a viable process for expressing sadness, we're left with no option but to suppress it. The suppression (prolonging) builds up over time and a simple emotion develops into a mood of general sadness. That melancholy mood once again gets prolonged, because we don't know what to do with it, so it becomes an attitude.

At this point, we'll have a predisposition to seeing things through sadness and will even use the word sad to describe any and all events that aren't positive.

'Isn't it sad that...'
'I feel sad that you...'
'Sadly, I had to resign before...'

People who are in this state will suck you inexorably onto their wave length and you'll begin to tap into your own sadness. Chances are, you'll feel like you're sharing their sadness.

If suppression (prolonging) continues, the sad attitude becomes a world view. At this point, everything is viewed sadly - the news, politics, the school system - and life turns into a series of sad happenings with brief moments of joy every now and again.

Just imagine what that same sequence looks like with fear...

As youngsters we were told not to be afraid and taught to hide it when we are, so the suppression starts early and builds easily. Fear quickly becomes an attitude - we watch out for strangers, car crashes, bullying, getting sick, mixing with the wrong people, being taken advantage of and even terrorist attacks.

Fear is prolonged and people often experience panic attacks - intense fear for no apparent reason. At this point, fear has become a way of life. Terror reigns supreme and we don't understand why.

In truth, we've come full circle. The fear that promised to keep us safe has progressed to the point that we live in a state of panic. Pushing the fear back by using calming techniques appears to work because the fear temporarily subsides, but there is no possibility of freedom until we address the situation properly.

NB: Beware of 'meditation as medication'. Meditation is very healthy, but be careful that you're not using it to suppress strong feelings that need to be expressed and released.

So, how do we address fear sequences?

In short, the quickest and easiest way through a prolonged fear sequence is to de-rail the pattern by working through the fears that are driving it.

Below you'll find another three fantastic techniques you can use to transform your fears and set yourself free.

The Crow Bar Technique

With this technique, the idea is to to gently 'lever out' one fear at a time. Here's how:

1. Imagine all of your fears (even the ones you are unaware of) as layers of wood nailed together in a vertical slab.

2. Bring one to mind - starting small. Imagine it as the top layer of wood in the pile.

3. Turn towards the fear and find where it lives in your body.

4. Explore the physical sensations and the emotion itself.

5. Mentally write the name of this fear on the piece of wood.

6. Ask yourself if you are prepared to let this fear go. Will you be safe without it? Will you be losing a close friend? Will you be alright after letting it go?

7. If the answer is positive, imagine a crow bar. Place the tip of the crow bar under the fear and gently lever it away from whatever it is attached to. Keep leaning on the crow bar - hear the nails squeaking as the layer of wood separates from the stack.

8. Imagine the fear separate from its origin, sitting there unable to attach to anything. Floating, disconnected and a bit lost.

9. Reverse the crow bar and hit the fear out of your body with the hooked end.

10. Watch it sail away and upwards eventually melting into the distance.

11. Breathe a sigh of relief.

The X Factor Technique

This technique is the one that seems to work best for both breaking 'bad' associations and banishing fear. We use it quite a lot in our clinical work when someone wants to stop something like smoking or biting fingernails. I'll describe it in that context first and then illustrate how it's easily applied to fears.

To quit something:

1. Close your eyes and imagine the thing you want to stop. Just bring to mind a picture of the packet of cigarettes or your fingers in your mouth.

2. Ask yourself what the cost of this indulgence has been in terms of money, friendship, or loss of self-esteem and put this together with the picture of the thing itself.

3. Place a big black X across the picture.

4. Imagine yourself peeling the big black X off the picture. As you do sirens erupt into deafening noise, the worst smell you have ever smelt arrives, lights flash and you start to feel as if you will vomit.

5. Visualise smoothing the big black X back down over the picture. As you do the noise stops, the smell goes away and your stomach settles.

6. Now surround the picture with a barbed wire fence and remind yourself that you never want to go there again.

7. Take a deep breath and open your eyes when you're ready.

To let go of a fear:

1. Close your eyes and imagine reaching a goal that would normally bother you. Perhaps you fear being lonely if you reach this target because people will leave you, so create an image of you all alone in the world, miserable and friendless.

2. Ask yourself what the cost of this fear has been in terms of money, self-confidence or friendships.

3. Place a big black X across this picture.

4. Imagine yourself peeling the big black X off the picture. As you do sirens erupt into deafening noise, the worst smell you have ever smelt arrives, lights flash and you start to feel as if you will vomit.

5. Visualise smoothing the big black X back down over the picture. As you do the noise stops, the smell goes away and your stomach settles.

6. Now surround the picture with a barbed wire fence and remind yourself that you never want to go there (imagining loneliness) again.

7. Take a deep breath and open your eyes when you're ready.

The 'Not That Thought' Technique

When we understand that thoughts create feelings, it's not difficult to see how most fears arise as a result of habitual thinking.

For example…

If I run across the road and crash tackle Fred, pinning him to the floor and breaking a rib, he'd have every right to feel attacked. But what if, a moment later, a bus crashes right where he was standing before I 'attacked'? My tackle saved his life, so is Fred now entitled to feel saved? Of course. But he has the same two broken ribs. When he was thinking 'attack' he felt one way, when thinking 'saved' he felt another.

It's easy to see why we say that one's thinking must be examined and cleaned up - it causes enormous problems if it isn't because we think in patterns that become habitual. Once they're habits, these processes happen so quickly that we don't even hear the thoughts as they whip through our head at the speed of light. Unfortunately, they produce the same result whether we notice them or not.

Changing thinking patterns can be incredibly tricky. Most people don't notice the thought and even if they do it's too late - the thought and accompanying feeling have already happened.

The Not That Thought technique comes from the Buddhist tradition. As you'd expect from thousands of years of refinement, it's startlingly simple yet amazingly powerful.

Here's what to do:

When a negative thought occurs, rather than battle with it, simply swat your hand in front of your face and say, 'not that thought'. Let the negative thought go by moving to the thought you'd have preferred to have in those circumstances.

This process requires less repetition that you'd imagine and I cannot recommend it highly enough.

FEARLESS

TWO HEADS ARE BETTER THAN ONE

Most of us suffer alone unnecessarily. The deep seated belief that our fear is something to be ashamed of causes us to hide it. Our assumption is that if others were to discover our fears they would judge us in the same way we have judged ourselves.

We also assume that the result of this judgement would be rejection. We fear that we will be treated with the same level of disdain that we have dished out to ourselves. This would leave us alone and friendless in a tough world. We fear that we may not survive and know at the very least we'd be lonely.

Unfortunately the consequence of hiding our fear is that we end up isolated and lonely anyway because we feel we have nothing worth sharing with others. The loneliness contributes to the feeling that there is something fundamentally 'wrong' with us.

Our judgement of ourselves extends to the idea that we should just 'get over it'. The fact that we have not been able to overcome our fears further convinces us that some key ingredient in being normal is missing.

The problem is with our assumption that we are flawed and will be judged. There are many more people prepared to display compassion and understanding than there are who would judge - but we haven't given them the chance to do so.

By hiding we cut ourselves off from any form of support, sometimes even when we know the support is there. Ironically, it turns out to be us creating the feelings of isolation and loneliness. This is precisely what that the fear promised you would not happen if you just kept quiet.

Alcoholics Anonymous is an excellent example to look at - you may recall we previously discussed how alcohol inhibits fear. Sufferers usually end up using AA as a last resort despite the fact that it has one of the most reliable track records in the world. It starts with admitting the problem out loud to a group of others who may judge and/or reject. It's highly unlikely that judgement will actually occur, but the first timer won't feel that way.

The focus is on telling the story of addiction and examining its effect over the years. This 'talking it out' is fundamentally important to the healing process. AA has a twelve step program that the willing undertake when they feel ready.

Open and frank communication with someone called a sponsor is a critical step in that program. This person has usually mastered their addiction and is willing to spend time and effort talking, advising, listening and most importantly sharing. Usually they spend more time listening than talking.

How does that relate to fear in general?

We can learn from what works in the real world and chief among the strategies used by AA is personal sharing of the situation. We've seen it countless times in group situations - the unburdening of a heavy emotional load always provides two much needed benefits.

The first is that the admitting of a fault or mistake allows the owner to bring that which is scary out into the light. Confession works as a wonderful catalyst in healing because the load is lightened and dealing with the truth allows us to search for solutions instead of spending all our energy hiding.

The second is that a crowd listening to a confession is almost certain to display compassion and understanding. When the person talking is expecting derision and judgement, it's a revelation for them to hear words of acceptance. It's difficult to describe the wonder of being admired for the courage to reveal what we consider ugly. Most crowds have an 'I've been there too' kind of response, which is astonishingly liberating for the person sharing.

Still, most people won't go to a group. They've already decided that it's full of people who are far worse than them and don't even want to think about going because doing so would cut painfully close to the bone. Often they'll be thinking things like, *"I just can't see how it could possibly help to spend all that time talking about it!"*

No matter how nervous it makes us, the truth is that any personal interaction with someone who has had similar experiences is going to be helpful. The internet has made it incredibly easy to dip a toe in - there are any number of groups you can join anonymously. A Google search would no doubt reveal something that suits within a few minutes.

Getting more personal (and therefore far more impactful) support is simply a matter of deciding what would work best for you. Here's a few options...

A Professional Coach

There are thousands of professional coaches out there. If you pick well they'll be highly trained and very experienced in their chosen field. Look for one who lists dealing with emotions and/or fear as a specialty. Check their testimonials and ask if they can have one of their successful clients give you a call so you can get a feel for how they work. Pay whatever they ask - if you pay peanuts you'll get monkeys.

A Sympathetic Friend

There are many people you already know who would be honoured to support you when you need some help. All of us have someone we respect and admire. Going to them and asking for help is often viewed by them as a mark of the respect you hold them in. People with calibre and quality are more likely to want to help than those who are struggling with life - so aim high.

It would be an unusual person who didn't suffer some sense of imposing - do not let this get in the way of your healing. If asking for help scares you, you may have to write to them because face-to-face is more than you can handle. Do it anyway - you'll be forever liberated by this act of courage.

A Fellow Sufferer

Perhaps the most perfect of all relationships is a mutually beneficial one. If you can find someone who identifies with the same issues, you can agree to help each other through it.

The main requirement is that you can build a strong enough relationship to allow you both to share your experiences. Hearing the similarities and differences in the way you both handle (or not handle) the situations you find yourselves in might be all that is needed to get a breakthrough.

If just plain talking it through isn't enough and you both feel the need to apply some kind of technique or strategy, this book is full of eminently suitable ones. Take turns at being the 'coach' and 'client'. Read straight from the book if it helps.

An Online Support Group

Once you have found a group, spend some time just checking things out as an observer. Keep an eye on the communication style - it needs to be consistently supportive and positive.

Once you feel safe, venture some small part of your story making sure to protect your privacy. If the feedback is helpful, venture further out into the open with more of your story.

It's of paramount importance that your privacy is protected at all times. Anything that goes into print can surface negatively years and years down the track so seek the support you need but be careful.

A Live Support Group

You may be ready to join a group that meets in person. If you are not ready now, when will you be? Chances are you're more ready than you think.

When you first attend, observe the group to make sure it's supportive and positive. Once you're satisfied with the nature of the group and the way it works, start going regularly and get involved.

Whatever you do - chose something from the list above and get on with it. Suffering by yourself is the slowest, most painful road to healing.

FEARLESS

WRITE IT OUT

By this point you've likely accepted the idea that overcoming fear is a matter of fixing things that have gone haywire in the subconscious. The problem then, is how do you communicate with a part of your mind that you are unfamiliar with regarding something that you have no idea about?

Despite extraordinary evidence that techniques like meditating, mindfulness and introspection reliably work, many people struggle to have confidence in them because they're a bit unusual. This means they are left without a process they can depend on.

Journaling is an excellent (highly under-rated) technique with a depth and effectiveness that tends to sneak up on people.

The benefits commonly stated by people who journal are:

- Opportunity to clarify thoughts and feelings
- Gradual sense of knowing yourself better
- Reduction of stress
- Improved problem solving ability
- Disagreements are resolved faster

- Discovery of an accepting, non-judgemental friend
- Increased creativity
- Finding your own truth
- Improved intuition
- Enhanced self-confidence

If you give journaling a go for a while and it works for you, the stages of the process will look something like this...

1. Small immediate benefits that are hard to define will pop up. Most people would say, *"I've got to get back to journalling - something positive is happening but I'm not sure what it is."*

2. The small benefits are gradually followed by much larger gains in terms of general peace, internal serenity, a more stable personality and a better outlook on life. This stage is described by most people as extremely rewarding in a way that can't be explained. As with mindfulness meditation, the benefits seem to magically appear as a consequence of the activity, not necessarily during the activity.

3. Journaling becomes a treat, a process you look forward to. It turns into a personal practice that is as rejuvenating as others like Yoga and meditation.

In short, journaling is an incredibly powerful process. Just don't expect fireworks and you'll no doubt come to love it.

Below are some guidelines for successful journaling.

1. Buy a solid book to write in. Some people like an expensive, special book while others prefer a notepad or exercise book. Just pick whichever works for you and get started. NB: If you think you're likely to resist writing in the special book for fear of messing it up, get something you wont have that worry with!

2. Dedicate a particular time of day to writing. Sit down with everything you need (cup of tea, pens, pencils) and commit to putting pen on paper. If your first sentence has to be, *"Hi, I'm Paul Blackburn and I have no idea what to write about - in fact I'm just sitting here wasting time..."*, that's fine - just start!

3. Write until your time has elapsed. This may have been ten minutes or thirty, but whatever it is, it's important that you stay focused and continue to write. Anyone who has done any serious journaling will tell you that it's that last five minutes that pulls the gems out of your subconscious. The commonly agreed to sweet spot is about twenty minutes.

Also, avoid:

• Waiting to hear the words form in your head before you put pen to paper

- Waiting for inspiration
- Hesitation and thinking it through
- Having to have it make sense before you write it
- Judgement - it kills the process
- Worrying about what others might think of your efforts if they read them

4. Don't worry too much about spelling and grammar. These are just going to slow you down and they don't contribute to the overall purpose of the exercise.

5. Write quickly. Doing so frees your mind to expel the deeply held concepts that may have trouble surfacing if they had to wait while your hand catches up. It can also be helpful to choose a theme or direction for the week.

6. Write not to make a record of your thoughts but to open a channel for your subconscious to express itself. You will be surprised and delighted at the myriad of understandings that suddenly reveal themselves to you - either as you go or in a sudden flash.

Understand that you can't predict what will spring forth from your subconscious, you can only give it the opportunity to do so. In doing so your subconscious will reveal much of what has previously been a mystery to you.

This worries some people enough to cause them to skip the process out of fear that it may reveal a deep seated desire to become an axe murderer or start robbing banks for fun. This is fair enough to the uninitiated, but by now you will have come to understand that you get to choose which things you act on and which you don't. A sensation or desire revealed is not a sentence to become that way.

7. Commit to not judging your efforts. The purpose of journaling is not to produce a piece of work for publication - in fact it's highly likely no one will ever see it.

The reason you would put the effort into journaling is the same as you would for meditation - it's quite possible it can be a thing that simply works for you. You'll know it's delivering when you can't explain exactly why but you feel better at the end of a journaling session than when you started. Like any other creative or expressive activity, it will take some dedication. You'll need to learn the mechanics of the process and perfect your technique - but the promise is as great as with any other creative endeavour.

If you're prepared to put in some time without any expectation of a result, the chances are extremely high that you will find some magic in the process.

If not - what will you have lost?

FEARLESS

THE OBSERVER

Close your eyes and ask yourself, 'Who am I?' When you get an answer like your name, occupation or relationship status say to yourself, 'Yes, that is what you do, but who are you?'

You'll get more answers that relate to your world and the way you participate in it. Keep asking, 'Yes, but who are you?' Continue with this exercise for about half an hour. You'll find that you are none of the things you tend to identify yourself with.

For example, you are not a school teacher. That is a job you perform. You may love it, even be uplifted by it, but school teacher is not who you are. No one loves you because of your teaching - they love you. They love how they feel when they are with you, that you care about them, challenge them, cajole them, encourage them and scold them. They love the inner you - the very one you're having trouble describing.

So who are you, really?

You are a spirit, a soul, an essence. The part of you that is not your body, your thoughts or even your feelings and is virtually impossible to describe with words - that's the real you. If you look deep within and spend time being introspective, you'll find that you are indeed no more or less than a presence.

Most of us are aware that there's two of us - the one riding the physical, mental and emotional roller coaster of life and the one just watching.

Of the two, which do you suspect is the real you?

The most real version of you is the one you'd call 'the observer'. Always there, always calm, peaceful and non-judgmental. It's vitally important that you get to know this 'real you' intimately. Your freedom depends upon it.

The observer (real you) sees everything that takes place in your life and watches you engage with it in ways that are no longer productive. It non-judgementally and emotionlessly observes the anguish, drama and effort knowing that you don't need to engage in this way. It merely observes that you do.

The observer possesses the world's most accurate picture of you - your behaviours, your actions and your words. It knows that you need to change, but has no desire to implement that change because desire would be an emotion. Equally, it has no resistance to you changing and realises you could be different in an instant.

To be successful with fear, you must to connect with this infinite part of yourself. The observer will free you from fear because it realises that everything is an illusion. It sees that your world is a whirlwind of stories, myths and legends you have made 'real'. It understands that your beliefs, actions and words are all reactions to a pile of drama you say is true, which is demonstrably not so.

The truth is that using the observer, you can let go of anything you choose to (even fear) in an instant. True learning is transformational, but relies on accessing the real you. The observer.

So, what does 'using' the observer look like?

It may be helpful to imagine the observer as an emotionless robot that accurately remembers and catalogues everything you have ever said or done. It will answer any question you ask but won't volunteer the information of its own volition.

If you were to ask the observer, "*What are my chances of meeting my commitment not to drink for the next month?*", it would emotionlessly reply with something incredibly accurate. You might hear something like, "*Zero. You have never made it past 18 days on any other commitment of this sort - your average number of days in these situations is 11."*

As a result, your subconscious (speaking through your intuition and emotions) will create a sense of unease about the commitment and your intellect will begin to rationalise why you may need to drop out early. Those two things combined undermine the commitment you've made to yourself and prevent you from being successful.

The observer functions on a higher plane and can therefore be useful in de-railing the intellect and emotions - but only if you learn to tune into it. To do that you'll have to make the time to regularly practice stillness.

If you're willing to turn towards the observer and ask it, *"Am I really suffering the loss I feel I am by not having this beer?"*, you give yourself the opportunity to rise above the noise created by your intellect and emotions. The truth is you're struggling because you're listening to the symptoms of the craving for a beer. If you begin to ignore them instead, they'll fade. The observer can help you see that in the blink of an eye, but only if you let it in.

The best way to use the observer is to imagine it like a person who fits into the role of coach or advisor. Each time you tune into the observer and ask it something, you'll realise that you are fine. You may currently be experiencing sinus pain or sadness due to a broken relationship, but the observer will allow you to see the stories you are telling yourself for what they are and then let them go.

When dealing with fear, the observer is an invaluable asset because it allows us to disconnect from the emotion and look at it honestly. The truth is that fear is based in the future - it's about something that might happen, not what is happening now. Our culture teaches us to stare our fears down, not question them. In fact, the last thing we are taught is that we should question the validity, veracity or power of a fear. Yet that's exactly what we need to do and using the observer is the best way to do it.

All you have to do to disconnect from fear is check in with the observer. Doing so will allow you to acknowledge that right here, right now, you are actually just fine.

Once you've done that, you can use any of the techniques in this book to process the fear and let it go permanently.

CASE STUDY

One of my favourite clients is a man named Rex Knowland. As a teenager, Rex was bright enough to wonder what life had to offer beyond what he saw around him. His country upbringing demonstrated nothing he aspired to. Working all day for 40 years to pay off a house and essentially become a robot held no appeal. He was bored in school and began to get into trouble. By 19 he was a full blown heroin addict staring down the barrel of a life of crime to fund his habit.

Stealing from others went against Rex's values, so he had his 'now or never' moment. He booked himself into the Salvation Army's farm facility for cleaning up addicts and 30 years later he's still a clean living, upstanding member of the community. He's even been on local government and charity boards.

Here's how he describes the decision to let something go...

"Withdrawal is what stops most people getting clean - they don't want to go through it. It's a gut wrenching, hair raising period but is manageable if you take a step back and understand day one is throwing up, day two is stomach cramps, day three is shaking, day four is an enormous headache and

so on. When you accept that, you can just get on with it." We'd call this using the observer.

Rex goes on to say, *"If I offered a million dollars in cash to anyone who would go through the process I described above, there'd be a ridiculously long line up of people because there's something worth the pain at stake. In my career as a public servant over 30 years, I earned in wages that million and more. Along the way I invested some of it and in retirement I've got a cash nest egg, investment properties, a share portfolio and some toys like a motor bike. I got all that in return for four unpleasant days. So when people tell me they can't move past something, I don't want to hear it. I say, 'Don't tell me you can't do it. Be honest - tell me you're a wuss and you won't do it.'"*

FEARLESS

COMMON **FEARS**, STUPID CURES

The most common fears are: fear of failure, fear of success, fear of death, fear of rejection, fear of ridicule, fear of loneliness, fear of pain and fear of the unknown. It would be fair to say that most other fears are versions of these ten. For example, a fear of spiders or heights triggers the feeling that we we may not survive. It's not so much the arachnids or heights themselves, but the consequences of being bitten or falling off the building. Hence, both are really a fear of death.

For each of the top ten fears, we're going to take a look at what's going on, examine the common 'cures' and then suggest some rational alternatives that will no doubt create better results.

FEAR OF FAILURE

What's really going on...

This fear is at the root of more problems than we have time or space to list. The main issue is that we tend to personalise failure. That is, failing an exam becomes an indication of lesser worth as a human being. Somehow we conclude that we're fundamentally flawed because we flunked a math or science test.

In some cases (particularly when we're young), we believe our parents will love us less and as such become ashamed of both self and performance. Shame makes us feel like we need to hide our flaws to prevent others judging us the way we have judged ourselves, which would be devastating.

When we need others to like us in order to feel good about ourselves, we'll do almost anything to gain that approval. Obviously, it's a downhill slide from there.

The common 'cure'...

By far the most powerful learning mechanism in our lives is to give something a go. Sadly, we fail to notice that almost everything we've learned up 'til now has been through trial and error. For example, chances are the first time you drove a car you weren't very good at it. It's undoubtedly true that you persisted with driving and became proficient. This is a classic example of failing your way to success.

As children, we just give things a go. Yet as adults, we expect to get it right the first time around and if we don't we either won't try again or dismiss ourselves as hopeless. The apparent cure for that is procrastination - if we don't try something, we can tell ourselves we haven't failed at it. Clearly, ninety-nine percent of procrastination is due to a fear of failure.

The common 'cure' is to become progressively less and less adventurous.

The real cure...

What we really need is a new, more positive relationship with failure.

As a long time coach of new entrepreneurs, I have lost count of the number of clients I've had whose main issue was not a lack of ideas but a lack of courage. The fear of pressing the 'go button' on a project and taking it live is palpable and shows up with comments like, *"I've just got to get a couple of technical issues sorted out before we can launch."*

Once my clients understand I will respect them more for a failure and less for procrastinating, things change dramatically. Therefore, it makes sense to think about who you look up to and respect.

What would they think of you holding back for fear of failing?
What would they say about a project you launched that failed?
What do you tell yourself about failure?
Is there a difference between the two views on failure? If there is, which one do you think better serves you?

FEAR OF DEATH

What's really going on...

The fear of death is a bottom line fear that creates many others. As we talked about at the beginning of the chapter, anything that makes us feel worried we won't survive really traces back to a fear of death.

For example, if you talk to someone who's terrified of speaking in public, you'll soon discover what they're really afraid of is being humiliated. Why? They think they won't survive it. So the thing driving the terror regarding getting up on the stage is actually a fear of death.

The common 'cure'...

We avoid talking about death because we can't cure it. This leaves us completely unprepared for one of the few things we can be certain will happen at some point. Most people are shocked when they recognise their own mortality. We remain generally unable to discuss this very important aspect of being human.

The real cure...

Get comfortable with your own mortality. Start as many conversations as you can about death and dying, spend time in a hospice and decide on your spirituality. Far too many people end up on their deathbeds regretting the way they spent their time on earth.

FEAR OF REJECTION

What's really going on...

We're taught that the acceptance of others is the lifeblood of our existence. That is, if we don't go out there and get enough approval, we will not survive. Therefore rejection by another (which may actually only be 'not being noticed') creates feelings of isolation, loneliness and struggle. We act as though others rejecting us or our ideas is fatal. In fact, it may be exactly what we need to let go of the neediness that characterises the search for approval.

Much of our behaviour is driven by the need to avoid offending people so they'll like us. The problem with that is that we subconsciously know those who accept us are doing so with limited information because we've kept them in the dark. Since we know we fooled them, we discount their acceptance and continue to experience the sense of rejection.

The common 'cure'...

We modify our behaviour to fit within the codes established within any group. This is one of the main reasons we experience being different with our family than we are with friends, at work or at the dog training club. By doing so we apparently save ourselves from rejection because we 'fit in'. Sadly, the price of fitting in is the gradual loss of self-identity.

The real cure...

The real cure for a fear of rejection is to explore and establish your personal identity from within. To do that, connect with your values and beliefs - once you can articulate these then your job is to spend your life living up to them.

Accept that you will be rejected at some point and understand that it is not personal. Rejection tells you more about the people doing it than it tells you about yourself.

FEAR OF RIDICULE

The fear of ridicule is very similar to fear of rejection, with one major difference. Ridicule is an extreme form of rejection - its main impact is to accentuate feelings of 'not being good enough'.

Proceed as with fear of rejection and be careful. Again, accept that ridicule will occur and it is not about you.

FEAR OF LONELINESS

What's really going on...

Loneliness is a very big problem in our culture. It tends to manifest with thoughts and feelings like, 'I'm on my own', 'No-one cares about me' or 'I must not be good enough to have friends'.

When we're experiencing those feelings, the problem of loneliness appears to be a lack of people in our life. Once again, after coming to the conclusion that we wouldn't be lonely if more people liked us, we attempt to fix the problem by modifying our behaviour.

In truth, that won't fix anything. Fear of loneliness is driven by being dependant on others for approval and connection. We worry that we won't be approved of or reaffirmed as a good person worthy of connection with others, which is a basic human need. This dependance on the approval of others is a problem - it means our sense of well being is derived externally rather than from within.

This fear is a version of the fear of death, in as much as we somehow sense that we will not survive on our own.

The common 'cure'...

Once again behaviour modification is the apparent answer. Our fear of being alone causes us to hang on to others, becoming needy and clingy. We even put up with substandard relationships so that we don't have to deal with our fear of being lonely.

The real cure...

By far the most effective treatment for a fear of loneliness is to form a healthy relationship with self so that one's own company can be enjoyed. Incidentally, as soon as the need to have people around disappears, the right ones will turn up.

When fear of loneliness pops up we're imagining a terrible outcome in the future, so living in the moment will also be an incredibly helpful tool.

FEAR OF PAIN

What's really going on...

This is another fear that really boils down to a fear of death. That is, we are certain the pain will be more than we can handle and as such we will not survive.

We claim to be far too busy to get to the dentist, but the truth for most people is that physical or financial pain is the real deterrent. This has to be imagined or remembered and is not actually happening yet. Again, we're projecting into the future. If your mother ever said, 'Just you wait until your father gets home' in a fit of anger, you'll be familiar with the anticipation of pain being just as unpleasant as the actual punishment.

Fear of pain can only be created when we believe we are our body. In reality, it is just the vehicle we are trapped in. Therefore pain is about the violation of our inner sanctum - our true self.

The common 'cure'...

The most common way of dealing with a fear of pain is to simply avoid it at all costs.

We go to extraordinary lengths to avoid pain - it's almost comical. We'll go to the drugstore, rather than the dentist. It's the imagination of pain at the dentist that keeps us away from them. Eventually the fundamental problem with the tooth means the pain becomes unmanageable and we're off to the dentist, where we should have been in the first place. We'll say something like, 'I don't care what you do, just stop this pain!'

The real cure...

We're so worried that turning towards the pain will make it worse that we avoid doing the only thing that will reliably work...

The way to deal with pain is to observe it. In doing so we can separate from it and thus control it.

Just ask someone with a chronic pain problem who is also allergic to pain killers - they'll tell you that turning towards pain and observing it dispassionately are excellent techniques for managing pain.

FEAR OF THE UNKNOWN

What's really going on...

This is perhaps the second most common fear, and again it traces back to a fear of death.

We've been taught to fear the unknown because we can't be prepared if we don't know what's going to happen. As a result, we're addicted to predictions about the future. Western cultures in particular are obsessed with knowing what will happen next.

We abhor the unpredictable - since clearly if we aren't prepared for it, we may not survive what comes next. For example, only about ten percent of people are willing to start their own business. Why so few? That's how many of us can deal with the unknown. Those who can't deal with it won't start a business because they need to know the pay packet will be there at the end of the week. They can't live with the idea that it may not, because, well...what would happen?

The common 'cure'...

We become control freaks who avoid unpredictable outcomes. We maintain hyper-vigilance because any number of things could go 'wrong'. Safety and conservatism come first. The cost of that is a complete lack of spontaneity - which generally means fun falls by the wayside as well.

The real cure...

The only solution to a fear of the unknown is to accept that we cannot predict the future. We don't even know if we will be alive tomorrow. Therefore it is imperative we let go of the ridiculous notion that we can predict anything, let alone effect the outcome.

The realisation that we have no idea what is going to happen in the future is a profound but necessary one. To be truly happy - you will need to acquaint yourself with the notion that we are clueless about the future. If you let it, this concept will set you free.

FEAR OF SUCCESS

What's really going on...

Most of us have noticed a rapid decrease in friends when we have an outstanding success. Either that or we have witnessed the stories being told behind someone's back when they succeeded. We notice that other people's success is not welcomed. In fact, we mostly see it being excused, derided or made fun of.

This triggers our fear of getting the same treatment from those we want to remain in relationship with. Therefore, fear of success is actually fear of being alone.

Success also carries its own burden - we are often afraid that we may have 'fluked' our initial success and the pressure to pull it off again is more than we can bear.

The common 'cure'...

Self-sabotage is the easiest way to avoid being successful, so we get right on with ruining our own chances. We'll lose concentration near the end of a project, deny we wanted something in the first place, get ready for failure and even be negative about success itself.

The real cure...

We don't need to be more successful. We just need to go up against the only person on the planet worth competing with - ourselves. Self-esteem is not built by winning, it is created by giving our best no matter the circumstances. We need to give it everything so that we can discover what we're really capable of.

Doing so also helps us to deal with possible failure. If we've given something our best shot and not succeeded, then we can learn failure isn't personal.

Just go for it.

FEARLESS

CONCLUSION

Chances are this book appealed to you because you recognised you're carrying fears you're ready to let go of, but you didn't know how.

You're now armed with the best set of techniques there are for working through fear. Using them you'll be able to live the life of your dreams, unhindered by your old fears. But that might be just the beginning...

We've established that every suppressed emotion lurks in the subconscious creating behaviours that don't serve you. But what happens if you leave those emotions unresolved for long periods of time?

Just like in nature, nothing remains static. Chop a tree down and return years later and you won't find a tree because it has morphed into something else. I believe the same happens in the subconscious with suppressed emotions - over long periods of time they change.

What do long buried emotions morph into?

Fear.

This explains why people who are bored or lonely can't help eating. Clearly, when eating becomes compulsive there's more at play than a lack of company or stimulation. What began as a simple desire for companionship or an inability to find inspiration gets suppressed and morphs into a powerful compulsion driven by fear.

Dealing with buried emotions using the techniques you're now equipped with isn't just good for you - it changes what drives your behaviour and in doing so, gradually alters your core beliefs for the better.

I commend you to the journey of discovery that this understanding can take you on. In fact, I hope you accept my challenge. That is, from this day on...

Do not bury anything at all. Instead, explore every emotion that arises for you. Do this when the emotion surfaces, while it is fresh.

Become capable of feeling your way through your 'stuff', because if you do, one day there will be no more stuff.

Warmest wishes for your journey within,
Paul

www.ingramcontent.com/pod-product-compliance
Lightning Source LLC
Chambersburg PA
CBHW040742020526
44107CB00084B/2845